# CRABTREE CONTACT

# MARTIAL ARTS LEGENDS

Clive Gifford

 Crabtree Publishing Company

www.crabtreebooks.com

# Crabtree Publishing Company

www.crabtreebooks.com          1-800-387-7650
Copyright © **2009 CRABTREE PUBLISHING COMPANY**.

**Published
in Canada
Crabtree Publishing**
616 Welland Ave.
St. Catharines, ON
L2M 5V6

**Published in the
United States
Crabtree Publishing**
PMB16A
350 Fifth Ave., Suite 3308
New York, NY  10118

Content development by Shakespeare Squared
www.ShakespeareSquared.com

With thanks to Dave Hazard and Bernard Rose,
and Bill Wallace and Rob (Mr. V) Vanelli.

Every effort has been made to trace copyright holders, and we apologize in
advance for any omissions. We would be pleased to insert the appropriate
acknowledgments in any subsequent edition of this publication.

**Author**: Clive Gifford
**Project editor**: Ruth Owen
**Project designer**: Simon Fenn
**Photo research**: Ruth Owen
**Project coordinator**: Robert Walker
**Production coordinator**: Katherine Berti
**Prepress technicians**: Samara Parent,
    Katherine Berti, Ken Wright

Thank you to
Lorraine Petersen
and the members
of nasen

**Picture credits**:
Alamy: Redchopsticks.com LLC: p. 7 (center)
Bernard Rose Photography: p. 9
Corbis: David Appleby/Buena Vista Pictures/Bureau L.A.
    Collection: front cover; Bazuki Muhammad/Reuters: p. 6;
    John Springer Collection: p. 12–13
Getty Images: p. 17, 29 (top left); AFP: p. 16, 20–21, 28;
    Popperfoto: p. 7 (bottom)
Gichin Funakoshi public domain: p. 8
Kodokan: p. 7 (top)
Rex Features: Everett Collection: p. 10–11, 19; Miramax/
    Everett: p. 18
RGA: Game of Death Concord Productions: p.15; Rocky IV
    Chartoff Winkler Productions: p. 14
Drew Serrano, East Coast Training Systems: p. 22–23
Shutterstock: p. 1, 2, 4–5, 8–9 (background), 16–17
    (background), 24–25, 26–27, 29 (top), 31
Morihei Ueshiba public domain: p. 24, 25
Courtesy of Bill Wallace, photography by Rob Vanelli: p. 14–15

**Library and Archives Canada Cataloguing in Publication**

Gifford, Clive
        Martial arts legends / Clive Gifford.

(Crabtree contact)
Includes index.
ISBN 978-0-7787-3776-6 (bound).--ISBN 978-0-7787-3798-8 (pbk.)

        1. Martial artists--Biography--Juvenile literature.  2. Martial
arts--Juvenile literature.  I. Title.  II. Series: Crabtree contact

GV1113.A2G53 2009          j796.8092'2     C2008-907858-6

**Library of Congress Cataloging-in-Publication Data**

Gifford, Clive.
  Martial arts legends / Clive Gifford.
        p. cm. -- (Crabtree contact)
  Includes index.
  ISBN 978-0-7787-3798-8 (pbk. : alk. paper) -- ISBN 978-0-
7787-3776-6 (reinforced library binding : alk. paper)
  1.  Martial artists--Biography--Juvenile literature. 2.  Martial arts--
Juvenile literature.  I. Title.  II. Series.

  GV1113.A2G55 2009
  796.80922--dc22
  [B]
                                                                                    2008052387

# CONTENTS

Martial Arts

Martial Arts Timeline

Gichin Funakoshi

Bruce Lee's Story

A True Legend

Superfoot

Steven Lopez

Jackie Chan

Ryoko Tani

Record Breakers

Morihei Ueshiba

Muay Thai Legends

Hadi Saei

Need-to-know Words

Martial Arts Words/
Martial Arts Online

Index

# MARTIAL ARTS

Martial arts were developed to be used in battle.

Most martial arts are types of hand-to-hand fighting without weapons.

Some martial arts are over 3,000 years old. Many were developed in Asia.

Judo

Some, such as judo, use holds and throws.

Others, such as karate and kickboxing, rely on strikes of the foot and hand.

Each martial art has different styles or schools. The Chinese martial art of **Kung Fu** has over 400 different schools.

Today, martial arts are used for self-defense, exercise, and recreation.

*Karate*

# MARTIAL ARTS TIMELINE

Here are some important events in the history of martial arts.

**Shaolin monks**
develop martial arts
Around 1500 years ago,
the first Shaolin monk
**temple** was built in
China. The monks began
to develop many different
martial arts.

*Chinese Shaolin Kung Fu monks*

## The invention of judo

In 1882, judo was invented by a Japanese man named Jigoro Kano. In 1909, Kano became the first Asian member of the International Olympic Committee.

*Jigoro Kano*

## Martial arts safety

Jhoon Rhee is a taekwondo master. He moved from Korea to America in 1956. In the 1970s, he invented the padded safety kit.

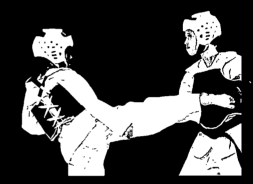

*Kickboxers in safety kit*

## Olympic Judo

Judo first appeared at the Olympics in 1964. Anton Geesink was the only gold medalist not from Japan. His success helped make judo more popular around the world.

*1964— Anton Geesink in action*

## Olympic taekwondo

In 2000, taekwondo became an Olympic sport.

# GICHIN FUNAKOSHI

Side thrust kick

Rooted stance with
high and low defense

Horse stance with
lower defense

Cat stance with
chicken wrist block

# BRUCE LEE'S STORY

Bruce Lee was the star of martial arts movies such as *Enter the Dragon* and *Fists of Fury*.

Lee's martial arts moves were amazingly fast.

Movie-makers had to use slow motion cameras so people could see his moves.

In 1973, Lee died suddenly. He was just 32 years old and very fit.

Lee developed his own martial art.
It is called **Jeet Kune Do**. It means
"the way of the **intercepting** fist."

# A TRUE LEGEND

## Bruce Lee could:

- Make a 1 inch (2.5 cm) punch which knocked a 220 pound (100 kg) man back 16 feet (4.9 m).
- Perform one-handed push-ups using just one finger and thumb.
- Pierce an unopened steel soft drink can using just his fingers.

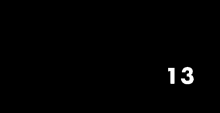

# MOVIE MAGIC

*Dolph Lundgren (right) and Sylvester Stallone in the movie,* Rocky IV.

*Chuck Norris with Bruce Lee in the movie,* Game of Death.

Taekwondo comes from Korea. Taekwondo means "the way of the foot and fist."

The first Olympic gold medal in taekwondo went to an American, Steven Lopez, in 2000.

Lopez followed it up with a second Olympic gold medal in 2004.

*Steven Lopez (in red) at the Beijing Olympics, 2008*

Lopez has family members that are amazing at taekwondo.

The Lopez brothers and sister all appeared at the 2008 Olympics.

*Steven Lopez*
*bronze medalist*

*Diana Lopez*
*bronze medalist*

*Jean Lopez*
*US team coach*

*Mark Lopez*
*silver medalist*

# JACKIE CHAN

Jackie Chan joined the China Drama Academy when he was just seven years old.

At the academy, Chan learned acrobatics, weapons training, and acting. He also learned wushu. This is a type of martial art that was invented in China in the 20th Century.

Chan's martial arts training helped him perform hundreds of amazing stunts in his movies.

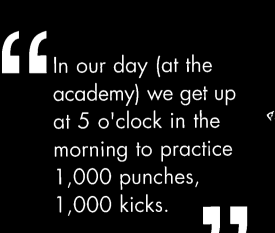

" In our day (at the
academy) we get up
at 5 o'clock in the
morning to practice
1,000 punches,
1,000 kicks. "

*Jackie Chan*

# RYOKO TANI

Ryoko Tani is only 4.79 feet (1.46 m) tall. She weighs less than 106 pounds (48 kg). Yet, she is the most famous and feared female **judoka** of all.

Why?

Tani has competed in five Olympic Games. She won a medal each time she competed.

Tani was just 16 when she won silver at the 1992 Olympics.

In the final of the 2000 Olympics, Tani won gold in just 40 seconds.

From 1993 to 1996, Tani was unbeaten in an amazing 84 judo **bouts**.

2004 – Athens Olympics final

Ryoko Tani

Frederique Jossinet, France

Some martial artists practice their striking moves on wooden boards and concrete blocks. This has led to some smashing records!

*Martial arts expert Drew Serrano makes a perfect "drop elbow" through a stack of concrete blocks*

**Fernando Camareno**
468 concrete tiles in one
minute (2007)

**Muhamed Kahrimanovic**
81 coconuts in one minute
(2007)

**Leif Becker**
487 wooden boards in
one minute (2005)

**Larry Fields**
354 concrete blocks in one minute
using elbow strikes (2004)

**Bob Knight**
3,014 wooden boards in
53 minutes (2003)

**Mike Reeves**
415 wooden boards in
one minute (2002)

# MORIHEI UESHIBA

Morihei Ueshiba was born in 1883. When he was young, he nearly died from scarlet fever. It left him a weak, feeble teenager.

Morihei Ueshiba

Ueshiba turned to **jujutsu** to regain his strength.

In the 1920s and 1930s, he developed a new martial art out of jujutsu. He called it **aikido**.

Aikido is mainly a system of self-defense. It uses an attacker's own energy to unbalance, **disarm**, and throw the attacker.

Ueshiba was just 5 feet (1.5 m) tall and weighed 110 pounds (50 kg), but he was a martial arts **legend**.

When he was 85, he gave an aikido demonstration.

Six young students attacked him at the same time. He sent his attackers flying with the smallest of movements.

Ueshiba in action

# MUAY THAI LEGENDS

Muay Thai is Thai boxing. This martial art is at least 800 years old.

Muay Thai is like kickboxing except you can use your elbows and knees to strike. You can also grab hold of your **opponent**.

# MUAY THAI LEGEND

Nai Khanom Tom was a warrior in Thailand. He was taken prisoner in a war between Thailand and **Burma**.

In 1774, he fought in Muay Thai bouts to gain his freedom. He beat ten fighters from Burma in a row.

King Mangra of Burma was so impressed he gave him his freedom.

# MODERN MUAY THAI LEGEND

Coban Lookchaomaesaitong is a modern Muay Thai legend. His nickname is "The Cruncher."

By the age of 15, Coban had fought over 35 times.

He won 250 out of 270 fights.

# HADI SAEI

Hadi Saei is a taekwondo champion. He started practicing martial arts when he was six years old.

Saei is the most successful sportsperson from Iran to enter the Olympics.

*2008 – Saei wins gold at the Beijing Olympics*

| Year | Olympics | Saei's Medal |
| --- | --- | --- |
| 2008 | Beijing | Gold |
| 2004 | Athens | Gold |
| 2000 | Sydney | Bronze |

In 2003, an earthquake destroyed much of the city of Bam in Iran.

Saei sold his taekwondo medals at an auction to raise money for the victims.

**aikido** A Japanese martial art which uses holds and other moves to use an opponent's movement against them. Many people learn it as a method of self-defense

**bout** A contest between two martial artists

**Burma** A country in Asia. Today, it is called Myanmar

**disarm** To make something or someone harmless

**intercepting** To take or hinder in the course of

**Jeet Kune Do** Martial arts invented by Bruce Lee. Martial artists use flowing movements, and stop an opponent's attacks with attacks of their own

**judoka** A person who practices Judo

**jujutsu** A Japanese martial art that uses throws and holds. Striking moves using tough parts of the body, such as the fists, are also used

**Kung Fu** The name given to a group of martial arts that came from China

**legend** A famous person who has become a hero to others

**opponent** The person you are competing against

**Shaolin monk** A monk (religious man) who follows the religion of Buddhism

**temple** A building for worship

# MARTIAL ARTS WORDS

All the martial arts may be different, but they have some things in common.

- **Accuracy**—You must perform your martial arts movements perfectly every time.

- **Discipline**—Keep control of your actions. Live and eat healthy.

- **Inner calm**—Learn to relax. Have your feelings under control at all times.

- **Practice**—Practice what you have been taught as often as you can.

- **Respect**—Always be polite and friendly to all teachers and other students.

- **Restraint**—Never use martial arts skills to attack.

# MARTIAL ARTS ONLINE

www.wkausa.com

www.gichinfunakoshi.com

www.ijf.org

www.wtf.org

**Publisher's note to educators and parents:**
Our editors have carefully reviewed these websites to ensure that they are suitable for children. Many websites change frequently, however, and we cannot guarantee that a site's future contents will continue to meet our high standards of quality and educational value. Be advised that children should be closely supervised whenever they access the Internet.

**A**
aikido  24–25

**B**
Becker, Leif  23

**C**
Camareno, Fernando  23
Chan, Jackie  18–19

**F**
Fields, Larry  23
Funakoshi, Gichin  8

**G**
Geesink, Anton  7

**H**
Hazard, Dave  9
history of martial arts
    4, 6–7, 8

**J**
Jeet Kune Do  11
judo  4, 7, 14, 20–21
jujutsu  24

**K**
Kahrimanovic, Muhamed
    23
Kano, Jigoro  7
karate  5, 8–9, 14
kickboxing  5, 14
Knight, Bob  23
Kung Fu  5, 6

**L**
Lee, Bruce  10–11,
    12–13

Lookchaomaesaitong,
    Coban  27
Lopez, Diana  17
Lopez, Jean  17
Lopez, Mark  17
Lopez, Steven  16–17

**M**
Muay Thai  26–27

**O**
Olympics  7, 16–17,
    20–21, 28–29

**R**
Reeves, Mike  23
Rhee, Jhoon  7

**S**
Saei, Hadi  28–29
self-defense  5, 25
Serrano, Drew  22
Shaolin monks  6
Shotokan karate  8–9

**T**
taekwondo  7, 16–17,
    28–29
Tani, Ryoko  20–21
Tom, Nai Khanom
    27

**U**
Ueshiba, Morihei
    24–25

**W**
Wushu  18